Fear

RESOURCES FOR BIBLICAL LIVING

Bitterness: The Root That Pollutes
Deception: Letting Go of Lying
Divorce: Before You Say "I Don't"
Fear: Breaking Its Grip
In-Laws: Married with Parents
Judgments: Rash or Righteous
Manipulation: Knowing How to Respond
Motherhood: Hope for Discouraged Moms
Problems: Solving Them God's Way
Self-Image: How to Overcome Inferiority Judgments

Fear

Breaking Its Grip

LOU PRIOLO

P&R PUBLISHING

P.O. BOX 817 • PHILLIPSBURG • NEW JERSEY 08865-0817

The author wishes to thank both Wayne Mack and Jay Adams, and to acknowledge the influence they have both had on his understanding of fear and its solutions from a biblical perspective.

Unless otherwise indicated, Scripture quotations are from the NEW AMERICAN STANDARD BIBLE®. Copyright © 1960, 1962, 1963, 1968, 1971, 1972, 1973, 1975, 1977, 1995 by The Lockman Foundation. Used by permission.

Italics within Scripture quotations indicate emphasis added.

Printed in the United States of America

Library of Congress Cataloging-in-Publication Data

Priolo, Lou.
  Fear : breaking its grip / Lou Priolo.
     p. cm. — (Resources for biblical living)
  Includes bibliographical references.
  ISBN 978-1-59638-121-6 (pbk.)
  1. Fear—Religious aspects—Christianity. 2. Fear—Biblical teaching.
I. Title.
  BV4908.5.P77 2009
  248.4—dc22
                        2009006257

HAVE YOU EVER been afraid? I mean *really afraid*. Not just a little scared but *terrified*. Have you ever been so filled with fright that you were absolutely paralyzed? Or, have you been so thoroughly possessed by fear that your body and soul seemed powerless to do anything against it?

The fear monster has gripped you by the throat, lifted you off your feet, and pinned you against the wall. There you are, dangling in the air, caught in his stranglehold, unable to breathe, unable to move, unable even to cry for help. As he squeezes your throat tighter and tighter, all you can do is look down at that stark, grotesque face of this monster called fear whom you dread more than almost anything else!

Perhaps you know exactly what I'm talking about. Or, maybe you have had milder encounters with the fear monster. You've seen him from afar and you respect him, although you've never been as utterly disabled by his paralyzing grip as I've just described. If you are reading this booklet, my guess is that you or someone you love has caught more than just a glimpse of him.

If so, I have good news for you: fear doesn't really possess you outwardly like the paralyzing grip of a monster. It is an emotion that you ultimately can learn to control (and you are responsible before God for doing just that). The fear monster *was born, resides,* and *must be slain—in your heart.* I would like to show you from the Word of God what you can do to slay this bogus bogeyman so as to keep him from terrorizing you.

Let's begin by briefly examining the place fear *should* have in your life. Fear, like every other emotion (anger, hate, and jealousy, to name a few), can be both constructive and destructive. It has power for *good* as well as for *evil*.

"But how can fear be constructive?" you wonder. Well, first, fear can keep you from *physical* danger (such as falling off buildings or going to jail or getting HIV/AIDS). Second, it can keep you from *spiritual* danger (such as falling into displeasure with God, exposing yourself to temptation, being brought into bondage by a life of dominating sin, being dis-fellowshiped by your local church, or being disqualified from ministry). Solomon said, "By the fear of the Lord one keeps away from evil" (Prov. 16:6).

If you are a fearful person, you undoubtedly have *some* idea of how destructive fear can be. It is essential, however, that you understand that above and beyond the misery that sinful fear produces, it is truly offensive to God.

So, at what point does fear become sinful? This is the question I would like us to consider next.

Characteristics of Sinful Fear

Fear is sinful when it proceeds out of unbelief, or distrust, in God.

When you are afraid because you do not believe that God *can* or *will* do what he has clearly promised in his Word, your fear is sinful.

> And in the fourth watch of the night [Jesus] came to them, walking on the sea. When the disciples saw Him walking on the sea, they were *terrified*, and said, "It is a ghost!" And they *cried out in fear*. But immediately Jesus spoke to them, saying, "Take courage, it is I; *do not be afraid*." Peter said to Him "Lord, if it is You, command me to come to You on the water." And He said, "Come!" And Peter got out of the boat, and walked on the water and came toward Jesus. But

seeing the wind, *he became frightened*, and beginning to sink, he cried out, "Lord, save me!" Immediately Jesus stretched out His hand and took hold of him, and said to him, "*You of little faith, why did you doubt?*" (Matt. 14:25–31)

Peter was afraid because he doubted. He distrusted God because his faith was small. Which promises of God do you sometimes not believe?

_____

_____

_____

Fear is sinful when that which produced the fear is attributed more power than what the Bible allows.

When you believe that what you fear has more power than God, your fear is sinful.

"I say to you, My friends, do not be *afraid* of those who kill the body, and after that have no more that they can do. But I will warn you whom to fear: *fear* the One who after He has killed has authority to cast into hell; yes, I tell you, fear Him!" (Luke 12:4–5)

Make a short list of the things that you fear. Think in terms of the following categories: your feelings, your enemies, your environment, your circumstances, your future, your finances, or the loss of your most cherished possessions.

_____	_____
_____	_____
_____	_____
_____	_____

7

Do you *really* believe that God is *bigger* than these things? If you really believed that God is omnipotent, you wouldn't be so frightened.

Fear is sinful when it attributes to God characteristics that are inconsistent with his nature.

When Christians are afraid, it is almost certainly because they have a misperception of God. Some people have what I refer to as the "Good Lord" mentality. These people can usually be spotted by their statements such as, "My God wouldn't send anyone to hell," or, "I'm going to sin and God is going to forgive me. No big deal!" These individuals probably don't fear God enough.

The other extreme is what I like to call "'The unmerciful tyrant' mentality." This is the view of God as a "cosmic killjoy" who not only shows little mercy and compassion on his children, but also makes it his goal to quash any happiness and fun they might experience. Hebrews 11:6, however, effectively refutes this view: "And without faith it is impossible to please Him, for he who comes to God must believe that He is and that *He is a rewarder of those who seek Him.*"

I appreciate what Samuel Bourn said in his discourse titled "On Religious Fear," published in 1760.

> All true fear of the Supreme Being can only spring from a right knowledge of him. And it consists, first and fundamentally, in conceiving and believing him to be what he is, most powerful indeed, but at the same time, most wise, just, and benevolent. . . .
> The character and title most constantly ascribed by our *Savior* and his *Apostles* to the Supreme being is *The Father*: and the appellation [or name] by which we are taught to address him, [is] *Our Father in heaven.* . . . But if we impute

to him qualities inconsistent with the *parental* character, and represent him to ourselves, as seeking and delighting, not in the happiness, but the misery and ruin of his creatures; we dethrone as it were, *the Father*, and set up in his stead *a tyrant*. . . . And the dread of such a false deity is widely different from the fear of God . . . producing timidity, distrust, dejection, horror and despair and leading to all the . . . corrupt methods, by which, men, deceiving themselves, may hope to appease his wrath and gain his favor.[1]

Do you think you have an accurate perception of God? At what points do you believe your perception might be inaccurate?

_____

_____

_____

To what extent do you really believe that the Lord will reward you for your faithfulness to him?

_____

_____

_____

Fear is sinful when we fear what God forbids us to fear.

Do not fear those who kill the body but are unable to kill the soul; but rather fear Him who is able to destroy both soul and body in hell. (Matt. 10:28)

1. Samuel Bourn, "On Religious Fear," *Discourses on Various Subjects of Natural Religion and the Christian Revelation*, vol. 2 (London: R. Griffiths, 1760), 356–57.

What is it that the Bible tells us not to fear? Here are three forbidden fears about which I regularly remind those I counsel:

The Bible forbids us from inordinately fearing people.

> The Lord is my light and my salvation;
> *Whom* shall I fear?
> The Lord is the defense of my life;
> *Whom* shall I dread?
> When evildoers came upon me to devour my flesh,
> My adversaries and my enemies, they stumbled and
>   fell.
> Though a host encamp against me,
> *My heart will not fear;*
> Though war arise against me,
> In spite of this I shall be *confident.* (Ps. 27:1–3)

> In *God* I have put my *trust;*
> I shall *not* be *afraid.*
> What can mere man do to me? (Ps. 56: 4)

> The fear of man brings a snare,
> But he who trusts in the Lord will be exalted.
>   (Prov. 29:25)

If you *fear* God you will desire to *please* God. If you inordinately fear *man* you will inordinately desire to please *man*—you'll be easily tempted to love "the approval of men rather than the approval of God" (John 12:43). Are there people in your life of whom you are excessively fearful? Who might they be?

_____

_____

The Bible forbids us from inordinately fearing our environment and circumstances.

> God is our refuge and strength,
> A very present help in trouble.
> Therefore we will not fear, though the *earth* should change
> And though the *mountains* slip into the heart of the sea;
> Though its waters roar and foam,
> Though the mountains quake at its swelling pride.
>   Selah. (Ps. 46:1–3)

> You will not be afraid of the terror *by night,*
> Or of the arrow that flies *by day;*
> Of the pestilence that stalks *in darkness,*
> Or of the destruction that lays waste *at noon.* (Ps. 91:5–6)

By night, by day, in darkness, and in light, *God is your environment!* He is everywhere; and everywhere he is, he is in control of your circumstances. Are there things in your environment or present circumstances about which you are afraid? What are they?

_____

_____

The Bible forbids us from fearing bad news.

> Light arises in the darkness for the upright;
> He is gracious and compassionate and righteous
> . . . .
> He *will not fear evil tidings;*
> His heart is steadfast, trusting in the Lord.
> His heart is upheld, *he will not fear,*
> Until he looks with satisfaction on his adversaries.
>   (Ps. 112:4, 7–8)

Fearful people often live in dread of receiving bad news. Be it through hastily scheduled meetings, telephone calls, correspondence through the postal system, emails, or instant messages, they anxiously await the hammer to fall on them. Their focus is on secondary causes—the Sabeans, the Chaldeans, the fire that fell from heaven (cf. Job 1:14–19), rather than on their sovereign heavenly Father who for his own eternal purposes causes all things to work together for their good. What kind of bad news are you dreading?

_____

_____

_____

Fear is sinful when it is rooted in the loss of some cherished idolatrous desire.

> Nevertheless many even of the rulers believed in Him, but because of the Pharisees they were *not confessing* Him, *for fear that they would be put out of the synagogue*; for *they loved the approval of men* rather than the approval of God. (John 12:42–43)

Why were these rulers afraid? They inordinately loved (idolized) the approval of man. Fear is the flip side of lust. Idolatry is like a coin—it has two sides: *desire* and *fear*.

Those who *lust after* money	typically *fear* poverty
Those who *lust after* approval	typically *fear* rejection and conflict
Those who *lust after* control	typically *fear* losing control
Those who *lust after* intimacy	typically *fear* loneliness
Those who *lust after* pleasure	typically *fear* boredom
Those who *love* their own life	typically *fear* losing it

What is it that you are most afraid of losing? (Write your responses on the lines below.)

_____

_____

_____

_____

_____

_____

_____

Later on, I will help you to determine whether there is any connection between your fear and your idolatrous desires.

Fear is sinful when it is so paralyzing that it keeps us from fulfilling our biblical responsibilities (loving God and neighbor as the Bible commands).

There is an interesting connection in the Bible between *fear* and *slothfulness*. In the parable of the talents (Matt. 25:14–30), Jesus likened the kingdom of heaven to a man who was about to take a long trip. He gathered his slaves and committed to them the management of his possessions. "To one he gave five talents, to another, two, and to another, one, each according to his own ability; and he went on his journey" (v. 15).

Two of the three went out and diligently invested their master's money. These men were rewarded among other things with the commendation, "Well done, *good* and *faithful* slave" (v. 21, 23). In contrast, the other man was reprimanded and called *wicked* and *lazy*. In the parable, *good* is the opposite of *wicked*, and *faithful* is the antithesis of *slothful*. Please notice in the pitiful excuse of the lazy slave the *fear* that apparently paralyzed him from fulfilling his responsibility.

And the one also who had received the one talent came up and said, "Master, I knew you to be a hard man, reaping where you did not sow and gathering where you scattered no seed. *And I was afraid*, and went away and *hid* your talent in the ground. See, you have what is yours." But his master answered and said to him, "You wicked, *lazy* slave, you knew that I reap where I did not sow, and gather where I scattered no seed." (Matt. 25:24–26)

People who are fearful tend to be lazy because they focus not on their responsibilities but on their fears. That which they fear distracts and even incapacitates them from faithful obedience. Even the proverbial sluggard is afraid to go outside because he says, "There is a lion outside; I will be killed in the streets!" (Prov. 22:13). And, as John tells us:

By this, *love* is perfected with us, so that we may have confidence in the day of judgment; because as He is, so also are we in this world. There is *no fear* in love; but *perfect love casts out fear*, because fear involves punishment, and *the one who fears is not* perfected in love. (1 John 4:17–18)

The apostle John develops the antithetical relationship that exists between fear and love. One is set over against the other. The context of this mutually exclusive paradigm is the future judgment of God. John is specifically addressing fear of the judgment of God in relation to his readers. He explains that to the extent an individual possesses both a love for God and the assurance of God's love for himself, fear of God's judgment will be expelled. He says, "If you know that God loves you and you know that you love God, you will not fear his judgment." He appears to be applying a general principle ("perfect love casts out fear") to a specific problem (the fear of judgment). The phrase "because fear involves punishment," which he also applies to this specific fear, seems to be another general principle. (Notice that he does not say specifically "fear of judgment" but simply "fear.") In other words, there is a broader application of this general principle than he makes in this particular context of future judgment.

There is nothing else in all the world—nothing in any man-made theory of counseling, nothing in any pill you can buy—that has the power to expel fear more effectively than biblical love.

"The one who fears is not perfected in love." To the extent that you are fearful, your love is incomplete or immature (it's not made perfect). Although the Bible records several emotions that Christ experienced, nowhere in the Bible will you find it said that Jesus was ever afraid! Why? Because the love that he possessed for the Father was absolutely and positively without question 100 percent perfect love.

This brings us right up to the next sinful expression of fear. But first, on the lines below, record any biblical responsibilities you have neglected to fulfill because of your fears.

_____

_____

_____

_____

_____

Fear is sinful when it is rooted in selfishness rather than love.

[Love] does not seek its own. (1Cor. 13:5)

There is an interesting correlation in the Bible between sinful fear and selfishness. People who are selfish *tend* to be fearful. People who are fearful are *necessarily* selfish. Perhaps the best way to demonstrate this is by studying the antithesis of both sins. According to 1 John 4:18, the opposite of (and remedy to) sinful fear is *love*. Look at it again: "There is no fear in love; but perfect love casts out fear, because fear involves punishment, and the one who fears is not perfected in love."

But, love is also antithetical to (as well as the antidote for) the sin of selfishness. According to 1 Corinthians 13:5, love "does not seek its own." It is not selfish. Try looking at it as an equation.

$$\frac{\text{Fear}}{\text{Love}} \quad \begin{array}{c} \text{is the opposite of} \\ \rule{3cm}{0.4pt} \\ \text{is the opposite of} \end{array} \quad \frac{\text{Love}}{\text{Selfishness}}$$

When love is factored out from both sides of the equation, the relationship between fear and selfishness becomes apparent.

$$\frac{\text{Fear}}{\cancel{\text{Love}}} \quad \begin{array}{c} \text{is the opposite of} \\ \rule{3cm}{0.4pt} \\ \text{is the opposite of} \end{array} \quad = \frac{\cancel{\text{Love}}}{\text{Selfishness}} = \frac{\text{Fear}}{\text{Selfishness}}$$

We can also demonstrate the same biblical relationship between fear and selfishness grammatically. Consider these definitions:

Love   is being more concerned with what I can *give* than with what I can *get*.

Selfishness   is being more concerned with what I can *get* than with what I can *give*.

Fear   is being more concerned with what I *might lose* than with what I can *give*.

Here is another way to diagram the relationship between (sinful) *fear* and *selfishness*.

$$\text{FEAR} \quad = \quad \begin{array}{c} \text{LACK} \\ \text{OF} \\ \text{LOVE} \end{array} \quad = \quad \text{SELFISHNESS}$$

Notice that while fear and selfishness are the sins of commission in this equation, lack of love for God and neighbor is the sin of omission.

Fear impacts the way we relate to others. Contrast the selfish, *taking* kind of thoughts of the fearful individual with those of a loving, *giving* person.

Fearful Person	Loving Person
"I wonder what he'll think of me?"	"I wonder what his needs are?"
"I'd better not let him get too close to me."	"Maybe I can be a good influence on him."
"If he gets too close, he'll realize I'm not perfect and then he'll reject me."	"What matters is not what he thinks of me but how I can minister to him."
"I've got to keep him from finding out about my problems."	"I wonder if he has any problem I can help him solve God's way?"
"I'll probably make a fool of myself."	"If I make a fool of myself, so be it. I'm more concerned about meeting his needs than I am about what he thinks of me."

How do these thoughts compare with your own? What do your thoughts reveal about you? Are you more of a God-pleaser or a man-pleaser? A God-pleaser is more concerned about fulfilling his God-given responsibilities or meeting the needs of others than he is about the potential

17

consequences of a particular action. He doesn't allow the thought of unpleasant consequences to keep him—paralyze him—from loving God and loving others the way a man-pleaser often does.

Guidelines for Conquering Crippling Fear

Before we move on, allow me to give you a word of caution. Please don't think that the remedies that you are about to learn will somehow magically transform your spirit of fear into a spirit of courage and tranquility simply by hearing or thinking about them. They will be effective only if they are worked deep into your soul each and every day over a period of time. As I sometimes tell my counselees, I do not have a magic pill for you to take, or "whiffle dust" to sprinkle over you that will quickly relieve your pain. But if you are willing to take your medicine, radically alter your diet, begin a program of daily exercise, and go to physical therapy three times a week (in other words, if you are willing to invest the time to do all that the Bible says to alleviate your fear), you can be cured of this dreadful sinful "disease."

Learn to obey the first and second great commandments.

> One of the scribes came and heard them arguing, and recognizing that He had answered them well, asked Him, "What commandment is the foremost of all?" Jesus answered, "The foremost is, 'Hear, O Israel! The Lord our God is one Lord; and you shall love the Lord your God with all your heart, and with all your soul, and with all your mind, and with all your strength.' The second is this, 'You shall love your neighbor as yourself.' There is no other commandment greater than these." (Mark 12:28–31)

I often ask fearful people if they are afraid of snakes, spiders, or rats. Typically I get a positive response on at least one of the three. Then I ask, "Well, suppose your little sister, daughter, or granddaughter was playing in the sandbox when all of a sudden you noticed a dreaded snake slithering up to her. What do you think you would do? Wouldn't your *love* for that little girl *overcome* (at least temporarily) your *fear* of snakes? Sure it would! You would get as close to that snake as would be necessary to rescue her.

"Or suppose you and I are taking a walk in a part of town we have never been to before. During our walk we pass in front of a home with a large picture window, behind which are a dozen people seated at a dining room table just finishing the final course of their family banquet. I say to you, 'Why don't you walk up to the door, ring the bell, and introduce yourself to that family of strangers?' Would you do it? Probably not. Why? Because you would be embarrassed to intrude on their gathering for no apparent reason.

"But what if I said to you, 'Look! The roof of their house is on fire!' At that point, your *love* for those total strangers would *overcome* your *fear* and you would run up to the door and crash their party!"

The most effective way to remove (put off) fear is to replace it with (put on) love. So to slay the fear monster in your life, you must make it your primary goal to please (love) God, rather than to expel your fear.

You must *obey God regardless* of your fear!

You must *love others regardless* of your fear!

Practically speaking, this means that in order to overcome fear you must also begin to change the way you talk to yourself about your fears. You must learn to focus not on the consequences of the action that you are afraid to take, but rather on the pleasure that your obedience will bring to

God and the ministry you will have to others. You may even have to pray a few prayers something like this:

> Lord, if I have another fearful or painful experience, *I'll just have to endure it*. I'm going to trust you to do what is best for me. I'm going to obey you *regardless* of the consequences. I'm going to love others *whether or not I* experience pain or fear by doing so.

Several years ago, I had the privilege of befriending a dentist. When the need arose to have a couple of my wisdom teeth removed, I began shopping for someone to perform the "molarectomies" without also taking my arm and my leg. My friend's price was by far the best offer I was able to find, so we set an appointment for the surgery. I had occasion to speak to my friend several days later and asked him whether he was going to anesthetize me for the operation, or whether he had an anesthesiologist in house. He explained that he wasn't planning on giving me *any* general anesthesia but only several injections of lidocaine.

Now what was I going to do? He was my friend, and I had committed to the surgery. How could I get out of this without insulting him? My lifelong fear of dentists wasn't making the decision easier. I decided to trust God and let my friend do the surgery.

So there I was in the dreaded dentist's chair awaiting, as dentists like to put it, the "discomfort" (i.e., PAIN!) that was sure to follow. But was I afraid?

No! In the days preceding the surgery, I had been thinking about how to apply 1 John 4:18 to my dentophobia. I decided that when I was in the chair, rather than focusing on the "discomfort" I was going to experience, I would focus on being the best molar extraction patient my friend had ever had. I was going to study his facial expressions in anticipation of what he was going to do next so that I might open my mouth wide enough and position my head at just the right angle so as to make his job easier. I was bound and determined to love my friend (neighbor) instead of fearing pain. Well, it worked! Even when one of the molars broke in two and the dentist had to replace the corkscrew he was utilizing to facilitate the extraction with a hammer and chisel! My love for my dentist overcame my fear quite effectively. (Of course, the Valium he gave me forty minutes before the operation probably didn't hurt any either.)

Fear is God's built in *alarm*[2] system to let me know that I do not love God and others as the Bible says I should. I cannot emphasize enough that the key to solving this problem of sinful fear is to train yourself to focus more on what you must put on (love) rather than what you put off (fear).

There is another illustration I like to use when explaining the put-off/put-on dynamic to my counselees. Taking hold of a glass that sits next to a pitcher of cold water on my desk, I say, "This glass represents your heart." After filling the glass halfway with water, I continue, "If I wanted to empty this glass in such a way that would make it difficult for someone to come along and refill it, I'd have to do more than simply empty it. What I'd do is begin filling the glass with something heavier than the water—such as little pieces of sand or perhaps another dense fluid such as Liquid Plumber." As I add the heavier substance to the water, it sinks to the bottom of the glass. As the glass begins to fill from the bottom, I ask, "What is going to happen to the water?"

"It will be displaced and begin to spill out over the top of the glass," comes the typical reply.

2. The word for *fear* both in English and in Greek could be translated *alarm*.

"That's right! And so it is with the sin in our life. We displace the sin in our heart *by* replacing it with something better—something "biblically heavier" if you please—than the sin."

Take a scriptural tranquilizer.

We don't hear the word *tranquilizer* used very often these days. It has been replaced by the terms *anti-anxiety* or *anxiolytic* medication. I prefer *tranquilizer* because of its association with the word *tranquility*. The Word of God has tranquilizing power.

> Those who love Your law have great peace,
> And nothing causes them to stumble.
> (Ps. 119:165)

> The steadfast of mind You will keep in perfect *peace*,
> Because he trusts in You. (Isa. 26:3)

Sometimes my counselees who have been prescribed anti-anxiety medications bring in the prescription bottles for their tranquilizers. Almost invariably the directions on the bottle read, "Take as needed."

I know of a tranquilizer that is far more effective and safer than any medication known to man. This tranquilizer when taken during times of anxiety and fear has even been known to begin working before most tranquilizers can be absorbed into and distributed throughout the bloodstream.

A spiritual tranquilizer consists of memorizing portions of related Scripture at the first onset of emotional distress. As soon as you become fearful, begin searching for and internalizing those exact portions of the Word of God that speak to your specific fear. "When [at the time] I am afraid,

I will put my trust in You" (Ps. 56:3). The impact of reading Scripture during times of distress is quite powerful. But the tranquilizing effect of memorizing and meditating on the appropriate portion of Scripture during those times is typically much more powerful.

The book of Psalms contains extensive material covering the broadest scope of human emotions. Whatever emotions you are capable of feeling, chances are you can find them identified in Psalms.

I will never forget a time of great anxiety in my own life. It occurred during my graduate training at a prominent Christian university. I was enrolled in a counseling theories class (where every student is exposed to a variety of the 250-plus secular and "Christian" theories of counseling). For three hours every Monday evening, I would be challenged by my professor and fellow students as to whether the Bible really was sufficient to help people deal with the working (non-medical) problems of life. I became rather anxious for fear that my view of Scripture was somehow wrong and that what I had believed about the Bible's ability to minister to man (apart from the aid of secular psychology) was erroneous. After all, most of my professors and many of my fellow students believed that Scripture must be supplemented with insights discovered by unbelieving theorists because they were convinced that the Bible *really* didn't have everything necessary for man to change.

Every Monday evening after class I would have to reach for a "spiritual tranquilizer." As I would sit for hours, reading, studying, memorizing, and meditating on portions of the Bible that spoke to the sufficiency of Scripture (i.e., Pss. 19; 119; 1 Cor. 1:18–2:16), it was as if the Holy Spirit poured oil into the wounds of my fearful, confused heart. Then, on the following Monday evenings, I would go back to class to defend the Bible, and return with a few more wounds. But each week as I would take comfort in the Scriptures, my fear was replaced by confidence and ever-increasing boldness. Finally the professor, whom I grew to love dearly, thanked me for my ministry in his life. Then he told me that he was going to change the way he would teach the theories course in the coming years and would subordinate his counseling theories to the teachings of the Bible, to help future students avoid such spiritual anxiety.

"What *time* I am afraid, I will trust in thee" (Ps. 56:3 KJV). At the *moment* of temptation, decisive measures must be taken. Here, as well, the instructions read: "Take as needed."

Meditate often on past occasions of God's faithfulness to you in all of your past dangers and distresses, and anticipate God's faithfulness being demonstrated in your present circumstances.

Charles Spurgeon said, "Faith has a good memory." A good memory is a tremendous weapon in the war against fear!

> Has God forgotten to be gracious,
> Or has He in anger withdrawn His compassion?
>> Selah.
> Then I said, "It is my grief,
> That the right hand of the Most High has changed."
>
> I shall *remember* the deeds of the Lord;
> Surely I will *remember* Your wonders of old.
> I will *meditate* on all Your work
> And *muse* on Your deeds. (Ps. 77:9–12)

> This I recall to my mind,
> Therefore I have hope. (Lam. 3:21)

A bloodhound that has lost the scent of its prey sniffs backward until it picks it up again. So when you become fearful, when you begin to lose hope and doubt that you will see the salvation of the Lord, *think backward* until you pick up the faith you lost along the way.

You may find it helpful to write out a list of those times in the past when the Lord has delivered you from the same or a similar set of fear-evoking circumstances and to carry that list with you so that you may have it always by your side as a memory jogger. On the lines below, write the first three "divine deliverances" that come to mind.

_____

_____

_____

Clear your conscience from all unresolved conflicts with others (both God and man).

> The wicked flee when no one is pursuing,
> But the righteous are bold as a lion. (Prov. 28:1)

The overwhelming majority of persons I've counseled who have been diagnosed as paranoid or schizophrenic by mental health professionals were excessively guilt-ridden individuals. As was the case with Adam and Eve, *guilt* is often at the root of fear.

> They [Adam and Eve] heard the sound of the LORD God walking in the garden in the cool of the day, and the man and his wife *hid themselves* from the presence of the LORD God among the trees of the garden. Then the LORD God called to the man, and said to him, "Where are you?" He said, "I heard the sound of You in the garden, and *I was afraid* because I

was naked; so I hid myself." And He said, "Who told you that you were naked? Have you eaten from the tree of which I commanded you not to eat?" (Gen. 3:8–11)

A person who lives in perpetual guilt lives in perpetual fear of punishment. That punishment may take the form of hell, of being exposed, of going to jail, of losing one's sanity, or of dozens of other consequences that are known to be the results of sinful behavior.

> By this, love is perfected with us, so that we may have confidence in the day of judgment; because as He is, so also are we in this world. There is no fear in love; but perfect love casts out fear, because fear involves punishment [torment], and the one who fears is not perfected in love. (1 John 4:17–18)

It's as if the Devil (the accuser of the brethren) has a little fear button that he can push to strike fear in the hearts of the guilty. When we live with a clear conscience toward God and toward man we are disabling that panic button and removing from our lives one of Satan's devices. Paul said, "I also do my best to maintain always a blameless conscience both before God and before men" (Acts 24:16). Are there any people with whom you have a broken relationship because of an offence that you have not made right? Who are they? (Write down their initials only on the line below.) Then purpose, by God's grace, to seek their forgiveness. If you are not sure how to do this, seek the help of your pastor or a biblical counselor.[3]

---

3. You may find a biblical counselor in your area by visiting the website of the National Association of Biblical Counselors, https://www.nanc.org, or by calling NANC at 317-337-9100. Also, a recording of "Clearing Your Conscience" (LP 11) is available from Sound Word Associates, 219-548–0933 (http://www.soundword.com/index.html). It will help in learning how to clear your conscience according of the Word of God.

*Consider the miseries and consequences associated with a life that
is paralyzed by sinful fear.*

Most Christians can see clearly the connection between
sinful actions and distressing emotions (i.e., the adulterer
who faces intense grief and loneliness because his wife left
him, the angry parent who has to deal with the guilt, sorrow,
and embarrassment of rearing a child who has been provoked
to characterological anger, or the Xanax-addicted wife whose
illegal "doctor shopping" has landed her in jail—isolated from
her loved ones). But many fail to consider the relationship
between sinful thoughts and the emotional misery such malefic
mental activity often brings. The Westminster Confession of
Faith puts it well.

> Every sin, both original and actual, being a transgression
> of the righteous law of God, and contrary thereunto, doth,
> in its own nature, bring guilt upon the sinner, whereby he
> is bound over to the wrath of God, and curse of the law,
> and so made subject to death, with all miseries spiritual,
> temporal, and eternal.[4]

> Do not be deceived, God is not mocked; for whatever a man
> sows, this he will also reap. (Gal. 6:7)

We often think of our thoughts as being very distinct
from our behaviors. But from God's point of view, thinking
is a form of behavior—it's an action of our minds. As such,
it has the capability of being sinful. Sinful thinking carries
consequences: "The backslider in heart will have his fill of
his own ways" (Prov. 14:14).

4. M. H. Smith, ed., *Westminster Confession of Faith* (Greenville, SC: Greenville
Theological Seminary Press, 1990; published in electronic form by Christian Classics Foundation, 1996).

Here are a few miserable side effects for you to consider as further deterrent to giving in to fear:

1) It is a sin that offends your loving Heavenly Father.
2) It produces guilt, anxiety, and depression.
3) It damages your body.
4) It hinders your witness for Christ.
5) It causes you to waste time and lose eternal rewards.
6) It robs you of confidence, faith, love, thankfulness, peace, joy, happiness, and sleep.
7) It keeps you from fulfilling your biblical responsibilities.
8) It hastens the very thing that is feared.[5]

Perhaps you can come up with a few more of your own.

_____

_____

_____

_____

_____

_____

Identify and remove idolatrous lusts from your heart.

John Flavel said, "The more you are mortified, the less you will be terrified. . . . It is the strength of our affections, that put so much strength into our afflictions."[6]

5. Job says (in 3:25), "For what I *fear comes upon me*, And what I *dread befalls me*." Take, for example, a person whose fear of being rejected tempts him to withdraw from conversation and speak only when spoken to. This, in turn, tempts those around him to shy away lest they make him even more uncomfortable than he appears to be.

6. John Flavel, "A Practical Treatise on Fear," in *The Works of John Flavel*, vol. 3 (Carlisle, PA:, Banner of Truth Trust, 1968), 295.

As there are two sides to a coin, so there are usually two sides to idolatry. The first involves neglecting God. The other involves replacing him with a cheap substitute. The "heads" side says, "Inordinate Desire for Something." The "tails" side of the coin says, "Inordinate Fear of Losing Something."

The more you want something, the greater will be your fear of losing it. People who love money fear losing their wealth. Those who love to be in control fear being unable to control the circumstances and people who surround them. The person who loves pleasure is often afraid of missing out on opportunities to gratify his fleshly desires. For a people-pleaser, love of man's approval is typically accompanied by fear of losing someone's approval (or respect, or favorable opinion), fear of being rejected, and/or sometimes even fear of conflict. Chances are there is some inordinate desire on the flip side of your fear. "Little children, guard yourselves from idols" (1 John 5:21). What is it that you desire so much that the thought of losing it strikes terror in your heart? On page 13 I asked you to catalogue the things you are most fearful of losing. Review that list for a moment and then prayerfully read the inventory below, checking off any desires that have enticed you to sinful fear.

- ☐ I want to be healthy
- ☐ I want to be safe
- ☐ I want to be clean
- ☐ I want to be comfortable
- ☐ I want to be happy
- ☐ I want to enjoy myself
- ☐ I want to feel important
- ☐ I want to have a good reputation
- ☐ I want to be successful
- ☐ I want to be perfect
- ☐ I want to have wealth

- ☐ I want to have peace
- ☐ I want to have comfort
- ☐ I want to be alone
- ☐ I want to be thin
- ☐ I want to be in control
- ☐ I want companionship
- ☐ I want others to look up to me
- ☐ I want him/her to be my friend
- ☐ I want to avoid a conflict
- ☐ I want everyone to like me
- ☐ I don't want to be labeled
- ☐ I don't want to be rejected
- ☐ I don't want to face his/her anger
- ☐ I don't want people to know I'm such a sinner
- ☐ I don't want to have a panic attack
- ☐ I don't want to die
- ☐ I don't want to lose my spouse/children
- ☐ I want/don't want _____
- ☐ I want/don't want _____
- ☐ I want/don't want _____
- ☐ I want/don't want _____

Now that you have identified your idolatrous desires, ask the Lord for the wisdom, the grace, and the desire to dethrone them!

Remember that whatever makes you afraid has no power independent of God and therefore is powerless to do anything without his permission.

So Pilate said to Him, "You do not speak to me? Do You not know that I have authority to release You, and I have authority to crucify You?" Jesus answered, "You would have no authority over Me, unless it had been given you from above. . . ." (John 19:10–11)

> For the wrath of man shall praise You;
> With a remnant of wrath You will gird Yourself.
>   (Psalm 76:10)

John Flavel put it this way:

> Enemies, like wild horses, may prance and tramp up and down the world, as though they would tread down all that were in their way; but the bridle of providence is in their mouths, and upon their proud necks, and that bridle hath a strong curb [restraint].[7]

Another thing you may find helpful, having first identified the specific fears with which you are struggling, is to internalize specific portions of Scripture that address those fears (take a few more scriptural tranquilizers). On the chart below are a few examples to get you started.

"But," you say, "My problem is not that I doubt God's *ability* to control everything in my life and protect me from harm. My problem is that I doubt He is going to do *for me* what I believe he is capable of doing!"

What is it that you fear?	
That which I fear. . .	. . . is in God's control
Your Enemies	**Psalm 23:5** You prepare a table before me in the presence of my enemies.
Your Authorities	**Proverbs 21:1** The king's heart is like channels of water in the hand of the LORD; He turns it wherever He wishes.
Trouble and Affliction	**Psalm 34:19** Many are the afflictions of the righteous, But the LORD delivers him out of them all.

7. Ibid.

Trials and Temptations	1 Corinthians 10:13 No temptation has over-taken you but such as is common to man; and God is faithful, who will not allow you to be tempted beyond what you are able, but with the temptation will provide the way of escape also, so that you will be able to endure it.
	2 Peter 2:9 The Lord knows how to rescue the godly from temptation.
Poverty	Psalm 34:9–10 O *fear* the LORD, you His saints; For to those who *fear* Him there is *no want.* The young lions do lack and suffer hunger; But they who seek the LORD *shall not be in want* of any good thing.
Physical Harm (*people with phobias*) God is able to protect us from both *physical* and *spiritual* harm.	Psalm 91:5–7, 10–12 You will not be afraid of the terror by night, or of the arrow that flies by day; of the pestilence that stalks in dark-ness, or of the destruction that lays waste at noon. A thousand may fall at your side and ten thousand at your right hand, but it shall not approach you. . . . No evil will befall you, nor will any plague come near your tent. For he will give his angels charge concerning you, to guard you in all your ways. They will bear you up in their hands, that you do not strike your foot against a stone.
Loss of a Loved One (*or the effects of one's own death on a loved one*)	2 Corinthians 1:8–10 For we do not want you to be unaware, brethren, of our afflic-tion which came to us in Asia, that we were burdened excessively, beyond our strength, so that we despaired even of life; indeed, we had the sentence of death within ourselves so that we would not trust in ourselves, but in God who raises the dead; who delivered us from so great a peril of death, and will de-liver us, He on whom we have set our hope. And He will yet deliver us.

Welcome to the club! For most Christians—especially those of the Reformed persuasion—the difficulty is not the *sovereignty* of God, but rather the *goodness* of God.

To help such doubting believers, I often unpack 1 Co-rinthians 13:7, showing how it should apply to our love for God in view of his goodness to us: "[Love] believes all things." This means that, in the absence of hard evidence to the contrary, love believes the best about others—it puts the best possible interpretation on the facts. In other words, if there are ten different interpretations for an individual's choice of a particular course of action, nine of them being evil and only one being good, love will reject the nine and believe the one. If you and I are commanded to view fellow sinners with this kind of optimism, how much more should we interpret God's dealings with us in the best possible light? How much more ought we forsake our gloomy interpretations of his providence in our lives and accept the good ones? What's more, if God does allow you to experience torment by your enemies, abuse by your authorities, poverty, or whatever else you are afraid of, it is only because he intends to bless you with the happiness that comes with being conformed to the image of his Son!

Contrast the faithfulness of God with that of your dearest and most faithful friend.

There is a friend who sticks closer than a brother. (Prov. 18:24)

I would like you to think about and describe in the space below the one person in your life who over the years has been your dearest and most faithful friend.

_____

_____

_____

Now evaluate the extent to which you could trust your friend with your life or welfare were it totally in his hands.

_____

_____

_____

Next, answer this question, "To what extent can I depend on my friend to help me when I am in need, in prison, in sickness, in pain, in distress, or in danger?"

_____

_____

_____

Finally, compare the love, loyalty, resources, and wisdom of your dearest friend with that of your heavenly Father.

_____

_____

_____

_____

_____

_____

Do you really believe that your most faithful friend—the sinner that he is—is worthy of more trust than your loving heavenly Father? If you can trust your closest friend to be loyal to you, how much more should you trust the infinite faithfulness of him who loved you from before the foundation of the world, who redeemed you, who pledged himself to you, and who promised to work all things together for your good?

Learn to distinguish between fear of the object and fear of the experience.

> For if you cry for *discernment*,
> Lift your voice for understanding;
> If you seek her as silver
> And search for her as for hidden treasures;

Then you will *discern the fear of the* LORD
And discover the knowledge of God.
    (Prov. 2:3–5)

In the final analysis, it is not generally a particular object (bridge, airplane, elevator, etc.) that a person fears, but rather, he fears the recurrence of a painful experience he once had while associated with that object. While on a bridge or plane, while in an elevator or similar enclosure, the phobic individual may have experienced fear. From that point forward, when he sees or even thinks about a bridge, plane, or elevator, he associates it with that fearful experience and anticipates having another fearful experience.[8] This association and anticipation are the essence of his fear. Jay Adams explains the progression.

> You remember a fearful event in the past; let us say that you hallucinated in a crowd. . . . The experience was terribly frightening and very embarrassing. Even now as you remember it, you begin to become slightly afraid. You think: "I don't ever want that to happen again." As you think about the possibility, you recognize that it *could* and you begin to become *afraid that it will*. What is happening? You are becoming afraid by becoming afraid that you will become afraid. You feel the fear coming over you and this makes you afraid that you are going to have another fear experience, which triggers a higher level of fear that you now sense and that makes you even more afraid, and so on, and on, and on. . . . Do you see how it cycles? You did not know at that time that your hallucination was due to significant sleep loss . . . so when the hallucination occurred in a crowd you associated it with crowds—the association was possible particularly because of the great fear and embarrassment that it aroused. Now you take every precaution to stay away from crowds *for fear of*

8. When my daughter Sophia was a toddler, for example, she would complain, "My tummy hurts when we ride on the freeway!"

bringing about another fear experience (i.e., to say this precaution is fear-motivated). Indeed, the more precautions that you take, the more concern that you show, the more fearful such a situation becomes. And the more that you avoid crowds, the more fearful they become to you. The more you concern yourself with such things, the more you produce fear. It is not the crowds that produce fear—crowds do not have that power. *You* fear; but you fear the crowd because you have had fear experiences in relationship to crowds (those since the original one have been brought on in crowds as you feared that you would fear when in a crowd). The crowds do not cause fear; it is your fear of fear that causes it. Crowds *remind* you of your past fear experiences in crowds, and you fear having any more.[9]

Rather than perceiving the fear for what it is in truth (a creation of his own imagination that is triggered by the thought or sight of some object, for which he is responsible), the fearful person perceives what it is in error: a monster over which he has no control that seizes him from outside his body and paralyzes him with debilitating horror. The truth is that you do have the ability to control what you think. As we will see in the next point, controlling fear involves controlling thoughts.

Consider the connection between fear and undisciplined thinking.

For God has not given us a *spirit of fear*, but of *power* and of *love* and of a *sound [disciplined] mind.* (2 Tim. 1:7 NKJV)

Have you noticed how so many of the guidelines for conquering fear mentioned to this point have to do with your thinking? We've looked at learning to *change the way you talk to yourself,* to *pray,* to *sooth your thoughts with biblical tranquilizers,*

9. Jay E. Adams, *What Do You Do When Fear Overcomes You?* (Phillipsburg, NJ: P&R Publishing, 1975), 6–7.

to *employ a God-focused memory*, to *consider consequences*, to *remind yourself of God's sovereignty*, to *anticipate God's faithfulness*, and to *distinguish between objects and experiences*. It is by disciplining your thoughts in these ways that you can and must conquer that monster called fear that inhabits your mind.

And don't forget that you must learn to work hard at correcting any misperceptions in your thinking about the character of God—especially those that cause you to distrust him (cf. Heb. 11:6) such as, "God is not really in control," "God is going to punish me," and, "God doesn't love me—he will not be merciful to me."

Start fulfilling those responsibilities you have been neglecting because you have been so preoccupied with fear.

Now that you understand that it has been your lack of love for God and neighbor that has paralyzed you, you must act on that knowledge. By God's grace you can begin to obey the first and second Great Commandments from Jesus—no matter how you feel. Don't let the monster you created in the laboratory of your own mind keep you from loving God and your neighbor. Commit yourself to fulfilling your God-given responsibilities *whether or not you have another experience with fear*. Here is some additional advice from a trusted source.[10]

> And as you set out in obedience to God, filled with the task at hand, thank the Lord for whatever progress you have made. Focus on the loving activities that you are going there to do, not upon the fear experience you are trying to avoid. Don't allow yourself the all-too-expensive luxury of thinking about the fear experience. Don't think about trying to stop it. Think about serving God and about using your gifts to help others.

10. Ibid.

Whenever you catch your mind wandering back into the forbidden territory (and you can retrain and discipline it to love) change the direction of your thought. Do not allow yourself one conscious moment of such thought. Instead, crisply ask God to help you to refocus upon those things that fit into Paul's list recorded in Philippians 4:8–9. The attitude must grow within you that says: "So if I have a fear experience, so what? It's unpleasant, it's disturbing, but I'll live through it—at least I always have before." When you honestly can think this way without becoming anxious, you will know that the change has been made.

On page 15 I asked you to record those responsibilities you have disregarded in deference to your fear. Now I would like you to prioritize them in order of biblical importance and then prayerfully begin to invest your time, effort, and thought into fulfilling them. It may not be easy at first. You may have to beat down the fear monster. But this time, because you are fighting with biblical weapons, you know he will run away.

Remember that you may not be able to accomplish each responsibility as efficiently as you could during your less fearful moments. But by God's grace you will now be able to do them. "I can do all things through Him who strengthens me (Phil. 4:13). In time, your efficiency should return.

Before I conclude, let me mention one final action point for you to prayerfully carry out.

Learn to live in the fear of the Lord.

This is the *bottom line*. This is the stream into which all of the other brooks and creeks run. This is the *one cure* for sinful fear to which all the aforementioned guidelines may be reduced. It is the *essential ingredient* of which all the other antidotes for fear are made.

> Come, you children, listen to me;
> I will *teach* you the fear of the Lord. (Ps. 34:11)

How does one learn the fear of the Lord? Deuteronomy 31:11–12 gives us a clue.

> When all Israel comes to appear before the LORD your God at the place which He will choose, you shall *read* this law in front of all Israel in their hearing. Assemble the people, the men and the women and children and the alien who is in your town, so that they may *hear* and *learn* and *fear* the Lord your God, and be careful to observe all the words of this law.

We learn the fear of the Lord by *reading* the Bible, *studying* the Bible, *memorizing* the Bible, and *meditating* on the Bible. One of the terms for Scripture is "the fear of the LORD." Check it in the italicized words in Psalm 19:7–11 below.

> The *law* of the LORD is perfect, restoring the soul;
> The *testimony* of the LORD is sure, making wise
>   the simple.
> The *precepts* of the LORD are right, rejoicing the heart;
> The *commandment* of the LORD is pure, enlightening
>   the eyes.
> *The fear of the* LORD is clean, enduring forever;
> The *judgments* of the LORD are true; they are righteous
>   altogether.
> They are more desirable than gold, yes, than much fine
>   gold;
> Sweeter also than honey and the drippings of the hon-
>   eycomb.
> Moreover, by them Your servant is warned;
> In keeping them there is great reward.

The fear of the Lord is something that can be learned from others. It is contagious![11] *The fear of God is the one fear that removes all others!*

> "I say to you, My friends, *do not be afraid* of those who kill the body and after that have no more that they can do. But I will warn you whom to fear: *fear* the One who after He has killed, has authority to cast into *hell*; yes, I tell you, *fear Him!*" (Luke 12:4–5)

It doesn't matter how much your life has been paralyzed by fear. You can *learn* the fear of the Lord. You can learn to fear him *more* than you have learned to fear the *impotent* and imaginary fear monster that has tormented you for so long! David said, "*When* I am afraid, I *will* put my trust in You" (Ps. 56:3). He made a *decision* to *trust* in God. How about *you*? Have *you* ever made a *deliberate decision* to learn to live in the fear of the Lord? If not, why not make one right now—before you put down this booklet.

---

11. Incidentally, the same is true of sinful fears. People often learn fear from others (especially from parents; cf. "Come, you *children*, listen to me; I will teach you the fear of the Lord." [Ps. 34:11]). I cannot remember the last time I counseled someone who was suffering from extreme fear or anxiety who did not have at least one parent who similarly struggled with worry or fear. Do you remember the two lies Abraham told about his wife because of his fear? His son Isaac apparently picked up the traits of fear and deceit from his father's example. Check out Gen. 26:6–7.